The CHRISTMAS HOUSE

The CHRISTMAS HOUSE

by *Ann Turner*

Illustrations by Nancy Edwards Calder

HarperCollins*Publishers*

Other Books by Ann Turner

Rainflowers

Through Moon and Stars and Night Skies

Stars for Sarah

Rosemary's Witch

Heron Street

The Christmas House
Text copyright © 1994 by Ann Turner
Illustrations copyright © 1994 by Nancy Edwards Calder
Printed in the U.S.A. All rights reserved.

Library of Congress Cataloging-in-Publication Data
Turner, Ann Warren.
The Christmas house / by Ann Turner ; illustrations by Nancy Edwards Calder.
    p.   cm.
Summary: A series of poems describe what Christmas means to various members of
a household—grandparents, parents, children, pets, and even the house itself.
  ISBN 0-06-023429-6. — ISBN 0-06-023432-6 (lib. bdg.)
1. Christmas—Juvenile poetry.   2. Family—Juvenile poetry.
3. Children's poetry, American.   [1. Christmas—Poetry.   2. Family life—Poetry.
3. American poetry.]   I. Calder, Nancy Edwards, ill.   II. Title.
PS3570.U665C48   1994   *93-12740*
811'.54—dc20   *CIP*
                                                                    AC

Typography by Tom Starace
2   3   4   5   6   7   8   9   10
❖

To Antonia Markiet—the heart of Christmas

—*A. T.*

For my parents

—*N. E. C.*

THE HOUSE

I am one hundred years
old this Christmas.
How many times my door has opened
and shut to those I love,
arms filled with presents.
I have had fires lit in my fireplaces.
I have had eight beds warmed
on Christmas Eve.
I know about children.
They never sleep that night.
My stairs know their quiet steps
before dawn,
when they creep down to see
the tree, tall and glowing.
My walls know the soft press
of fingers as children go up
the stairs to play in the attic.
My walls know the touch
of old fingers, holding on
as feet go down.
My attic knows those who are gone
and those who have just come.
My cellar knows coal and heat and dust.
I welcome them all,
I hold them all,
I gather them in,
and I let them go
at the end.

CAT

This is a strange season.
No one sleeps.
Everyone eats.
They talk too loud,
they laugh too much,
they made a boat from my bed.
Someone brought a dog,
a black-and-white horror
who chased me upstairs
under the bed, where I spat
and hissed until the mother
rescued me.
The baby sucked my fur.
The girl dressed me in red
and put me in a pram.
The boy set off a Chinese cracker
too near my ear.
But the grandfather remembered
and put down pieces of turkey
and a spoonful of gravy.
Soon it will be over
and I can go back to my bed,
the quiet house,
the warm fire.

NICKY

Did they remember the rocket?
Did they remember the chemistry set?
You never know if you'll get
just what you want,
and you have to keep
your face just so
when you open the present and it isn't
what you hoped for.
Once I got a book about bridges.
My face felt like a lemon,
but I smiled still. We mustn't
disappoint them, Mother says.

I couldn't sleep Christmas Eve.
I crawled into bed with Peter,
and he rolled and turned
in the dark
while I stared at the light
under the door.
I heard the rustle of paper,
their feet going downstairs,
Dad's complaint
about putting together
Annie's new dollhouse.
I can hardly wait.
I'll get up at five and sneak
downstairs to touch the packages,
to see what pokes over
the top of the stockings.
I'll probably never sleep.

ANNIE

Christmas began with cousins—
eleven of them piling
out of the packed cars
like too many clowns.
We raced up the stairs
to the attic
filled with boxes, clothes,
and the old dollhouse.
Jeannie and I tried on dresses
from long ago,
collars up to our chins,
sashes tight at the waist,
with buttons small as mouse eyes.
In those dresses we felt
we could never be bad,
or run too fast or shout too loud.
We wore them downstairs
to Christmas dinner
and we were good,
and did not run too fast
or shout too loud.

Later, dressed in jeans,
I was sad for those
little girls in stiff dresses
who could not run or jump
on the rug in the hallway
with the laughter of aunts
all around.

PETER

Can't say
the word, too hard.
Lots of feet—
arms reach out,
a green smell.
Dog barking—
a bright light—
I cry.
Candy cane!
Suck on it
here
no hands to grab me,
no feet too near—
quiet.

MOTHER

The rush, the hurry
of shopping, cards,
visiting and food
and never enough time to sit
and think what it is all about.
But yesterday
we walked in the woods
to gather pine.
I knew then.
Utter quiet.
Birdsong.
The crunch of children's feet
on snow.
Armfuls of scented pine
hiding our faces.
Sunlight spilling
through the trees,
as it did so long ago
on a rough stable,
on a woman in a hurry,
on a worried man
soon to be at peace.

FATHER

Is this what it is
about? Saving money
all year so we can buy
toys, and baubles, and things?
I like stuffing stockings,
stringing the tree with
lights, welcoming them all
home again. But what else
is it?
Peter is learning to talk
this year.
Annie took her first ride
without training wheels.
Nick knows how to use
a microscope.
But where is the light
at the heart of Christmas?

The tree calms me,
green smell sharp inside,
the lights like tiny paths
showing the way,
and when we sit at the table to eat,
Grandmother will read grace,
glasses slipping on her nose,
and I know
I am at the heart
of Christmas.

AUNT

I've come all the way home
from Baltimore, with four children
and a dog in back,
one of them carsick.
I am glad to be here.
The hallway smells the same,
of hats and gloves and pine.
You stand at the foot
of the stairs with your arms
outstretched. We hug.
The fireplace flames
are blue and green
from father's pinecones
and the children ooh and ahh.
I am older, you are older still,
but you are my parents,
these are the presents,
this is the always house
of the forever childhood
and I am happy
to be here.

THE TABLE

Careful with those dishes.
They are hot.
Put them on the sideboard,
with each appointed spoon.
Orange squash,
pearl onions,
a dish of celery,
mounded potatoes,
turkey cooked so long
it falls before the knife.
Dark gravy rich
and thick.
Then pies;
mince, apple, squash
with just a taste
of brandy, "Careful!"
Grandmother cried.

I remember you when you
were small and beat your spoon
upon my top. I remember you
when your feet jiggled, waiting
for dessert. I remember Grandfather
crying out, "I've sugared my coffee
twice!" Now all are here
where I hold your faces deep
inside my polished wood.

DOG

Every year
the same.
The long ride
in the car,
the heat makes me sleep.
The arrival—
shouts, cries,
children running,
the baby falls,
no one remembers
my water.
Every year I chase
the cat upstairs,
then sit under the table
to catch the scraps.
That is the best part
of this long, loud
day.

GRANDFATHER

You asked for a story
of Christmas long ago,
when ladies wore white dresses
under the mistletoe,
and oranges floated sweet and strange
in pink punch.
But most I remember
the hoop Grandpa gave me,
and how I rushed outside
in my stiff new collar to roll
it down the hill.
It bounced and spun
over the meadow
into the river, unfrozen still.
A cow stepped on the hoop,
and it was a Christmas
of tears.
Now hush. All is well
on this green and white day,
in the house where my
knees are your lap
and my story is your song.

GRANDMOTHER

I waited at the foot
of the stairs, my
smile arranged,
my heart beat fast.
Weren't they late?
Were they all right?
No one told me I would always
worry, even though they are
long grown. Now
Marion runs down the rug,
her footsteps quick
and light, as always.
Henny is taller than I
and warm as toast,
and Lucy is golden
as a summer afternoon.
The children storm up the stairs
to the attic.
The boys hide in the water tank,
and the girls step primly down
wearing our old dresses.
I will remember their footsteps
like rain.
I will remember their laughter,
like sun.
I will hoard it up
to take out in the quiet
season,
a feast of family.

THE HOUSE

My attic knows those who are gone
and those who have just come.
My cellar knows coal and heat and dust.
My beds remember their shapes.
My stairs know their steps,
my walls their fingers.
I welcome them all,
I hold them all,
I gather them in,
and I let them go
at the end.